DESIGNS
ON

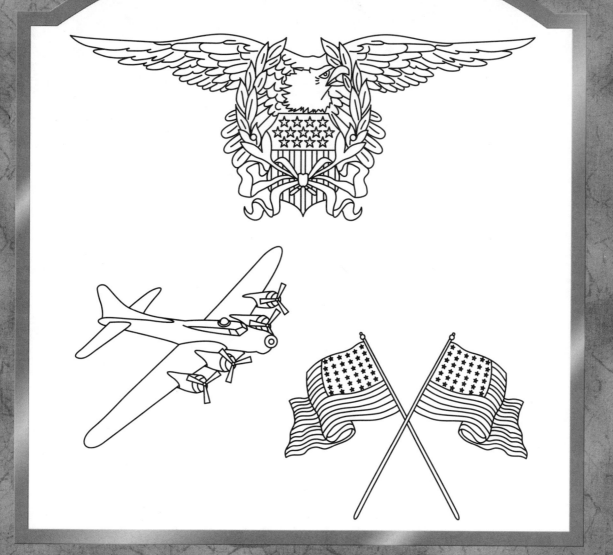

FREEDOM

Bonnie K. Browning

Located in Paducah, Kentucky, the American Quilter's Society (AQS) is dedicated to promoting the accomplishments of today's quilters. Through its publications and events, AQS strives to honor today's quiltmakers and their work and to inspire future creativity and innovation in quiltmaking.

BOOK DESIGN: LYNDA SMITH
COVER DESIGN: MICHAEL BUCKINGHAM
COVER PHOTOGRAPHY: CHARLES R. LYNCH

Library of Congress Cataloging-in-Publication Data applied for

ISBN# 1-57432-833-6

Additional copies of this book may be ordered from the American Quilter's Society, PO Box 3290, Paducah, KY 42002-3290, or online at www.AQSquilt.com.

Introduction

Throughout time, women have recorded the events around them—family history, community events, politics, and military conflicts—with needle, thread, and fabric. A group of women in Revere, Massachusetts, did just that during World War II. They made fifty quilt blocks with themes ranging from various aspects of the military to patriotic designs and the historic Boston area. For nearly sixty years, these blocks have wandered the country, traveling more than 6,000 miles—from Massachusetts, New Hampshire, Florida, California, and finally to Kentucky—rolled in an Almond Joy® box.

It is those blocks, and the inspiration behind them, that indirectly prompted me to develop this book of designs on freedom. The fifty quilt blocks were given to me by Doris Miller, from California, with the provison that I would assemble them into a quilt and exhibit that quilt. When the blocks arrived I was amazed at how much history and emotion of the times had been stitched into them. It was a history of the war in fabric. And, yes, they deserved to be made into a quilt.

Setting out to find fabric for sashing and borders was not an easy task. In fact, when the right colors could not be found, I contacted Marcus Brothers Textiles and we developed a line of fabric that matched the reds and blues in these blocks, and also represented historically accurate patterns. The quilt top is now assembled and will soon be quilted and exhibited.

The designs on the quilt blocks are simple shapes with embroidered details. I wanted to share some of these designs—George Washington, Abraham Lincoln, Paul Revere, Uncle Sam, eagles, flags, and military emblems—and began working on a book. With recent events around the world, and the U.S. involvement in those events in mind, additional patriotic and military designs have been added so quilters, embroiderers, painters, and other artists can use them to record today's history in their work. Children can use these designs for coloring.

Thank you to Doris Miller, who started me on this journey; to Marcus Brothers Textiles, who joined me in developing good clear red, blue, and yellow fabrics to go with the quilt blocks; to Meredith Schroeder and the staff at the American Quilter's Society, who always help make my work better; and to all the brave men and women who work every day to give us the freedom we enjoy in the United States of America—the land that we love.

Design sources include: quilt blocks designed by Mrs. Emma Blume, Revere, Massachusetts; *American Historical Illustrations and Emblems*, 1988, Dover Publications, Inc.; U.S. Military emblems from the Internet; and original designs by Bonnie K. Browning.

THE STAR-SPANGLED BANNER

U.S. Capitol

Designs On Freedom – *Bonnie K. Browning*

6

Star & Crest

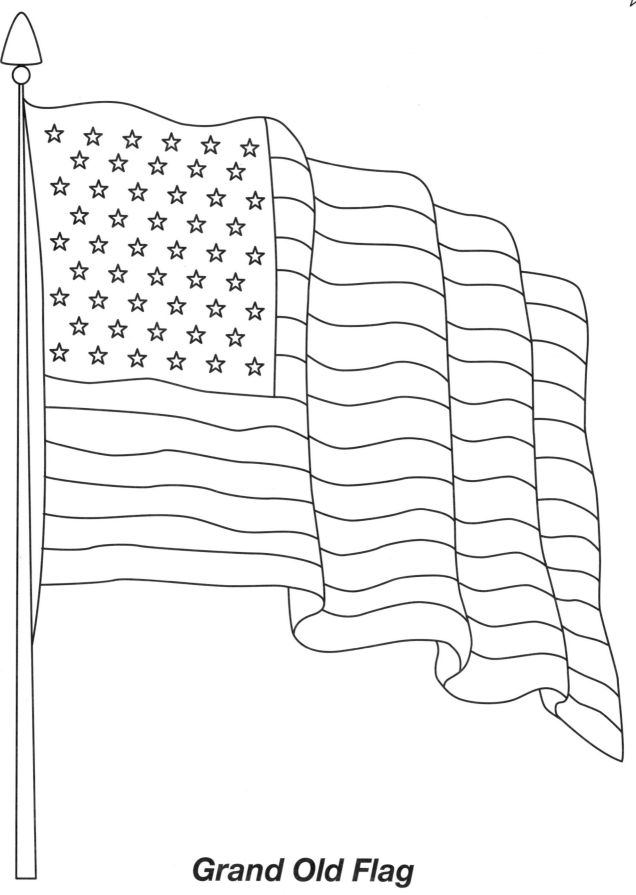

Grand Old Flag

Help is Always There

Designs On Freedom – *Bonnie K. Browning*

Old Glory

Designs On Freedom — *Bonnie K. Browning*

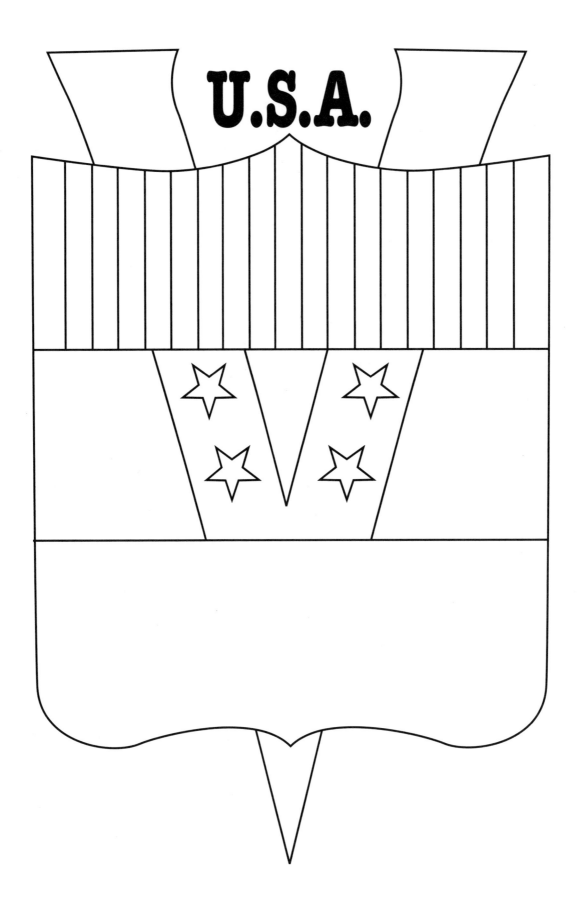

Buy U.S. War Bonds

Make a Five-Pointed Star with One Snip

Make a pattern for a five-pointed star in any size by folding a square of paper and making one single cut.

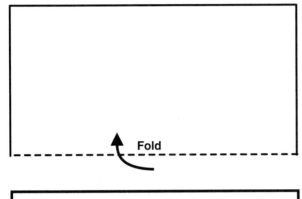

Step 1 Cut a square of paper the size you want the star to be. Fold the paper in half.

Step 2 Divide and mark the left edge of the folded paper into thirds.

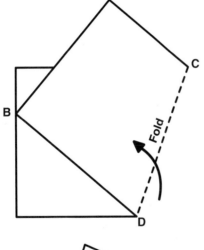

Step 3 Fold the lower right corner A to meet the upper mark B.

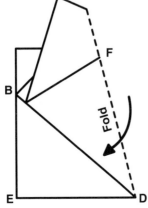

Step 4 Fold the CD edge to align with the BD edge.

Designs On Freedom — *Bonnie K. Browning*

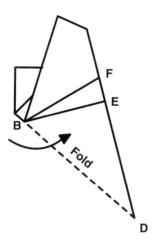

Step 5 Fold the bottom left corner E to the right to meet the DF edge.

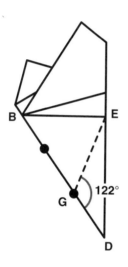

Step 6 Point D is the center of the star. Divide the BD edge approximately into thirds. Draw a mark at the lower third point to E. Fold to make a crease along the EG line. Open paper to check your star. Adjust the G point if necessary. When you are satisfied, cut along the EG line.

If you are making an appliqué pattern, add ¼" seam allowance to all edges.

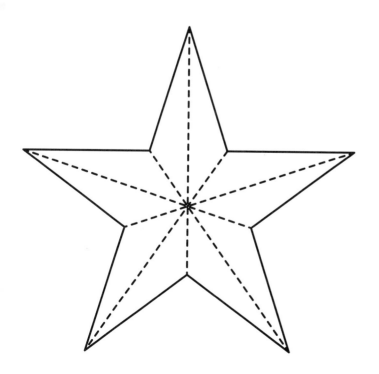

Designs On Freedom – *Bonnie K. Browning*

President George Washington

Honest Abe

Designs On Freedom − *Bonnie K. Browning*

LEXINGTON
CONCORD

One if by land, two if by sea

Hats off to the good old USA

Designs On Freedom – *Bonnie K. Browning*

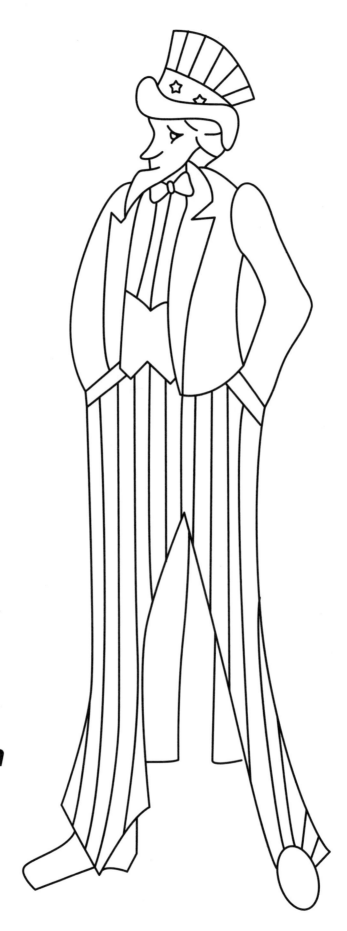

Uncle Sam

Designs On Freedom — *Bonnie K. Browning*

Uncle Sam Wants You

Designs On Freedom — *Bonnie K. Browning*

Fighting for Freedom

Designs On Freedom — *Bonnie K. Browning*

National Seal

Patriotic Eagle

Give Me Liberty

Designs On Freedom – *Bonnie K. Browning*

Peace Dove

Give Me Liberty

Designs On Freedom – *Bonnie K. Browning*

Proud and Regal

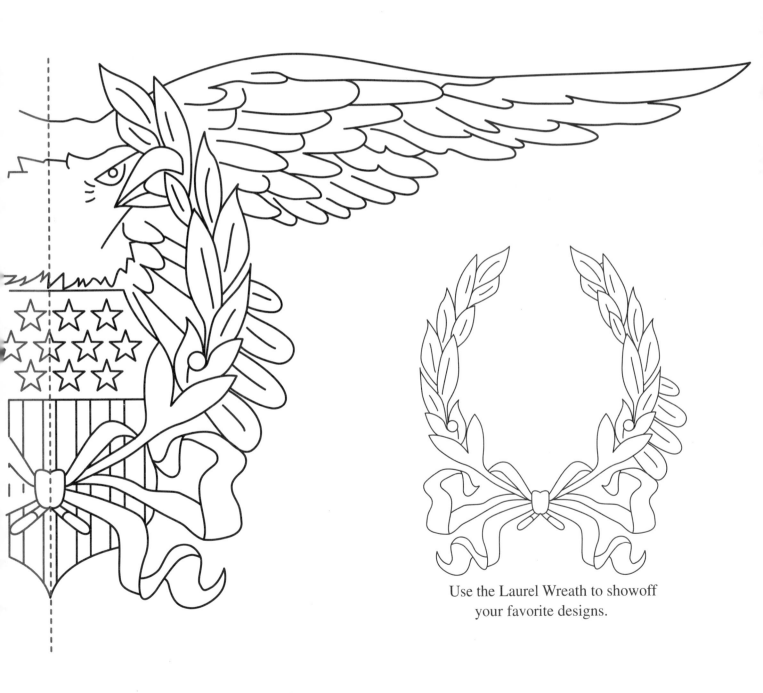

Use the Laurel Wreath to showoff
your favorite designs.

Designs On Freedom — *Bonnie K. Browning*

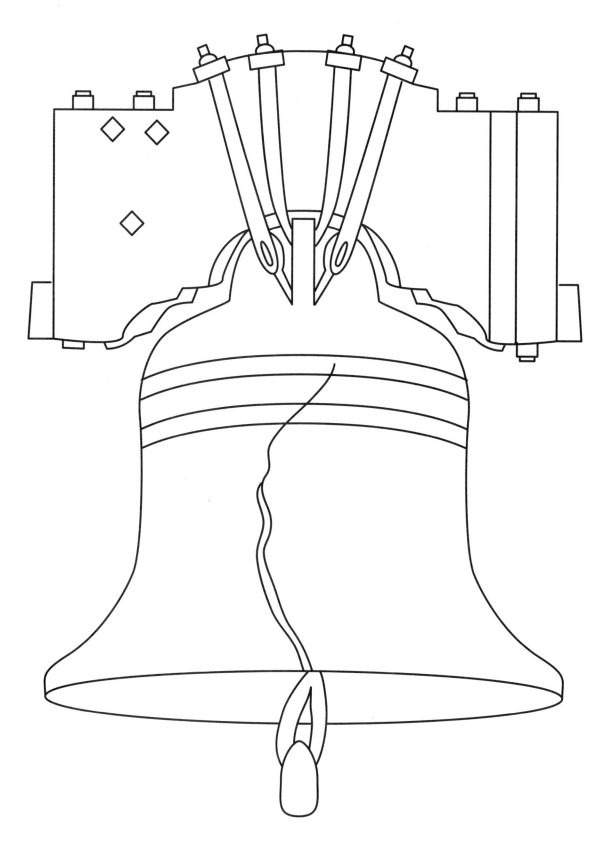

Ringing Freedom

Designs On Freedom − *Bonnie K. Browning*

Liberty and Justice for All

Designs On Freedom – *Bonnie K. Browning*

Protecting our Shores

GARDEN

FOR
VICTORY

Designs On Freedom – *Bonnie K. Browning*

Political Ups and Downs

Defending Our Great Land

Military Pride

Patches of Honor

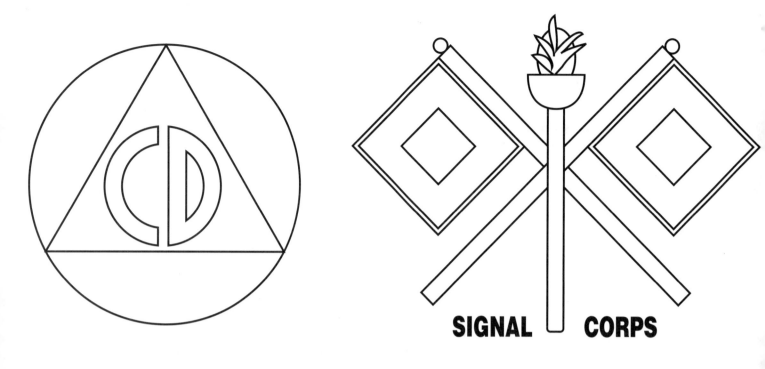

SIGNAL | CORPS

Serving Our Country

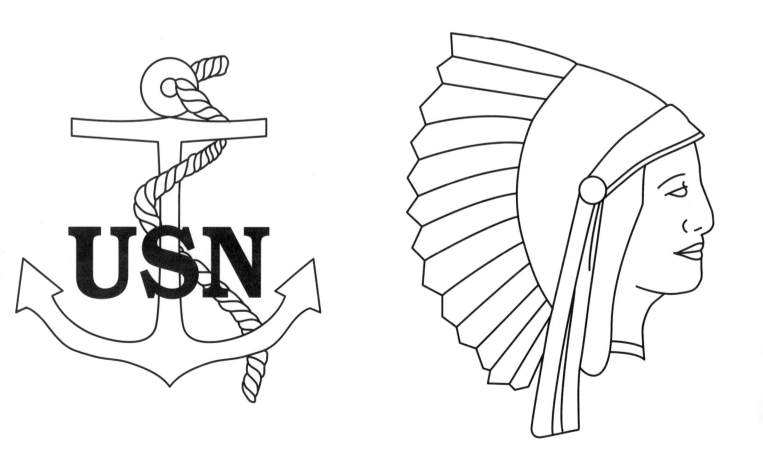

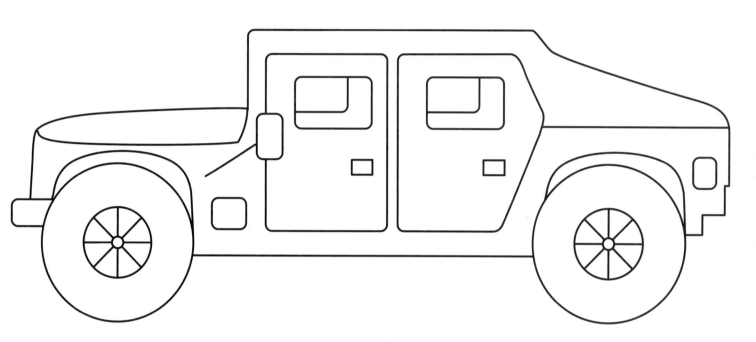

Military Vehicle

Designs On Freedom – *Bonnie K. Browning*

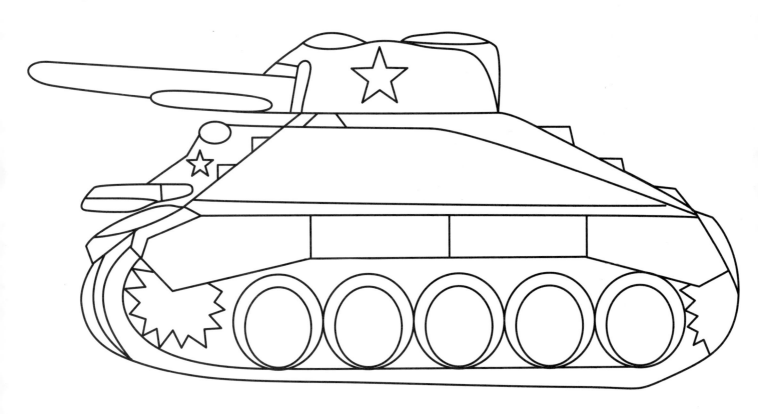

Sherman Tank

Designs On Freedom – *Bonnie K. Browning*

Medic

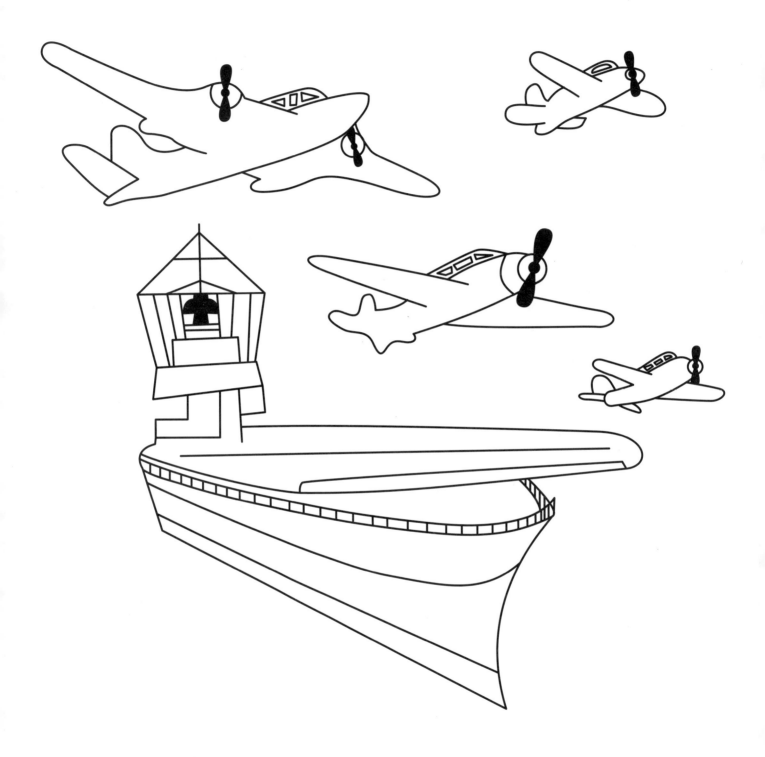

Battleship & Airplanes

B-17

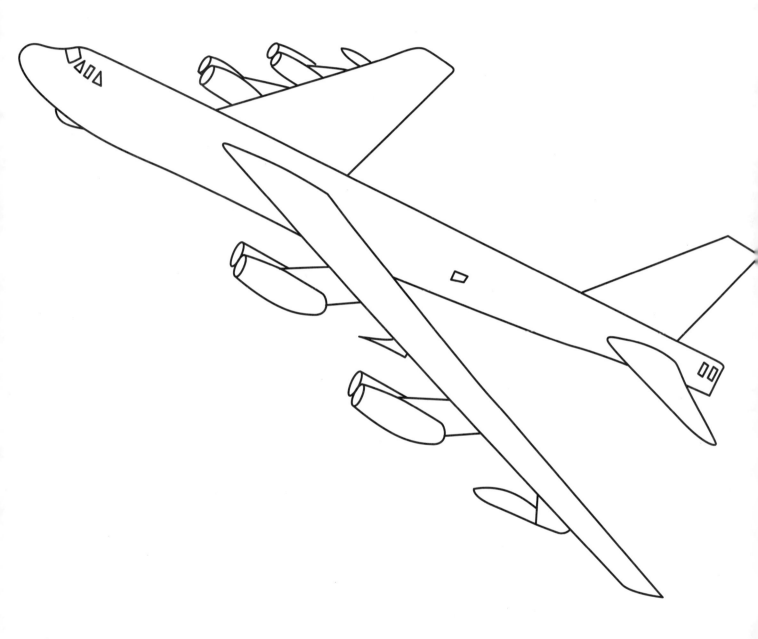

B-52 Bomber

Designs On Freedom – *Bonnie K. Browning*

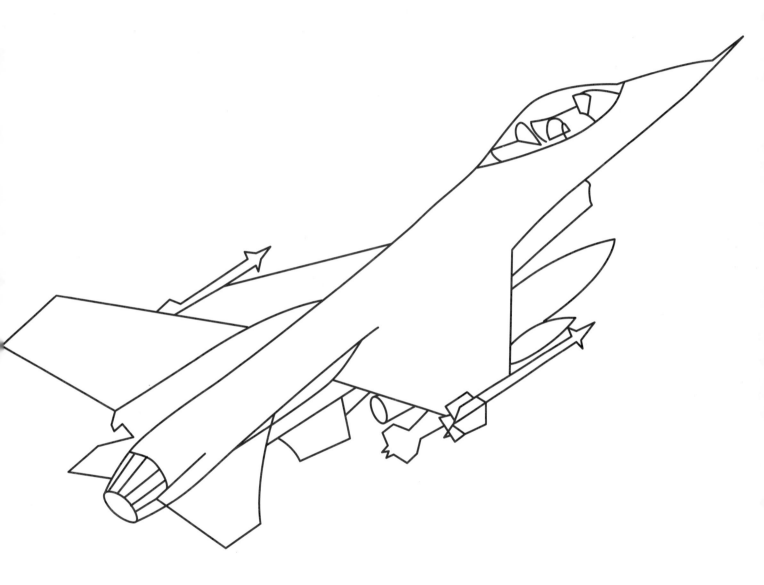

F-16 Fighter

44

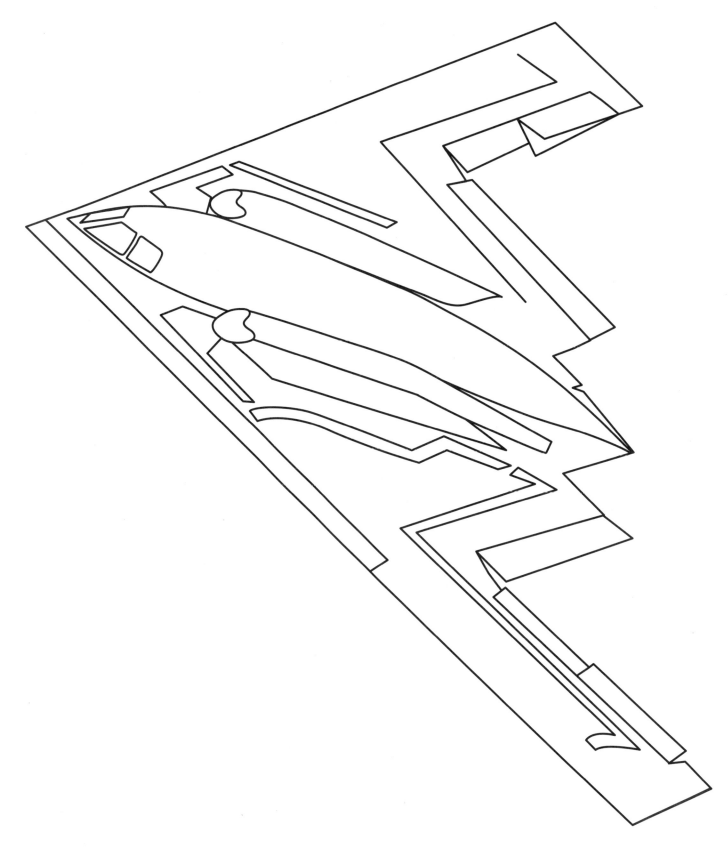

B-2 Bomber

Designs On Freedom – *Bonnie K. Browning*

Combat Helicopter

Designs On Freedom – *Bonnie K. Browning*

God Bless America

☆ ☆ ☆ ☆ ☆ ☆ ☆ ☆ ☆ ☆ ☆ ☆ ☆ ☆ ☆ ☆

Old Glory

United
We Stand

★ ★ ★ ★ ★ ★ ★ ★ ★ ★ ★ ★ ★ ★

Lady Liberty

FREEDOM

America
Land That
We Love